Light Between the Lines

JOY G. ARCAYENA

JOY G. ARCAYENA PUBLISHING

Contents

PART SEVEN
A FINAL BLESSING

Light Between the Lines:

Finding God in the Quiet Spaces

by Joy G. Arcayena

© 2025 Joy G. Arcayena

Ebook ISBN 979-8-9932573-0-3

Trade paperback ISBN 979-8-9932573-1-0

Hardback ISBN 979-8-9932573-2-7

For permission requests, write to: joygarcayena@gmail.com

"A good person leaves an inheritance for their children's children..."

— Proverbs 13:22

This book is my legacy—

a gift to my loved ones—

something to leave behind,

so they'll always carry a piece of my heart and faith with them.

Author's Note

I wrote this collection during a season of quiet stirrings, when I began to sense God calling me to write—to foster connection. Each poem and reflection carries a piece of my heart, a whisper of my prayers, and a deep desire to point others to peace, purpose, and the presence of God in the stillness.

This book did not come about through meticulous planning, but by paying attention to the gentle nudges of the Spirit. Each piece is personal, spiritual, and straight from my heart. While beginning to work on my memoir and devotional, I felt called to gather poems and reflections that had already taken root in my heart. These words—written across seasons of searching, stillness, and surrender—now feel ready to speak.

My prayer is that they meet you where you are and gently draw your attention to the quiet spaces where God is always present.

May you find yourself seen between the lines.

May you sense God's nearness in your own quiet spaces.

Thank you for joining me in these pages.

Joy G. Arcayena

Before the Poems Came

I was never the artsy one.

I don't cook, don't sew, don't sing, dance, or play an instrument.

I don't do crafts. I don't play sports.

Honestly, I've always felt a little out of place when people start talking about their hobbies or talents.

(My daughter, with love and humor, says I live in "La-La Land"—and I can't say she's wrong!)

But as I was approaching seventy, something shifted.

I was going through old papers—just purging—when I stumbled upon a few essays I had written in college, along with pages from years and years of journaling.

And suddenly... I remembered.

I remembered how much I loved words.

I remembered that English and literature were always my favorite subjects.

I remembered that I used to write.

It felt like opening a door that had been waiting patiently for decades.

And once I peeked in, I couldn't look away.

Not long after, I joined a Zoom open mic—by accident, really.

But that "accident" opened something else entirely:

Poetry.

I never thought I could write poems... but I did.

And something about it felt holy. Familiar.

As if God had planted that seed long ago—and it was finally time for it to bloom.

Could it be that what felt accidental was, in fact, divinely orchestrated?

Turning seventy became less about age and more about awakening.

These poems—these words—are just the beginning.

They are my offering. My joy. My testimony.

And now I know this much for sure:

It's never too late to rediscover who you are.

It's never too late to begin again.

It's never too late to become the person God has been gently calling you to be all along.

> *"For this reason I remind you to fan into flame the*
>   *gift of God, which is in you..."*
> — *2 Timothy 1:6*

PART ONE
The Call to Write

HOW THIS BOOK FOUND ME

I'd been caught up working on my memoir—trying to perfect it, pouring in days of effort. Then, out of nowhere, a new concept for a book came to me—something I hadn't planned. I'd been toggling between finishing the memoir and completing a thirty-one-day devotional, both of which meant a lot to me. But suddenly, I felt pulled toward something else entirely: to gather the poems and essays I had already written, to let them speak for themselves, and to build a book around them instead.

The urgency wouldn't leave me. I couldn't think about anything else but this new direction—completing it, shaping it, writing more about how I feel and how I've been led here.

One morning, while working out early, I was thinking again about my memoir—wondering how to structure it and when I'd carve out the time to do it. The devotional crossed my mind too—its purpose, its promise. But then came a quiet yet clear thought: What if I can do a mixture? What if I publish the poems and essays first?

I almost stopped mid-workout to write but told myself, "If I stop now, I won't come back to this." I value getting my workout done first thing, so I didn't stop. Still, the thoughts kept pressing in. I rushed through my routine—tried to finish it—but it felt like it took forever. Finally, I made it to my laptop and poured out what I was feeling before it slipped away.

And now? My mind is full—more thoughts, more poems, more essays, more questions to ask God. I'm praying for clarity, for grace, for guidance.

I guess what I'm trying to say is: I want to remember this moment. I want to capture the feeling of being called into something new and unexpected. If it comes to be, I want to trace its roots back to this moment—when the words wouldn't wait, and I chose to obey the nudge.

My goal is to publish a book. I want to accomplish something that matters. But more than that, I want to be faithful to the process—however it unfolds.

When the Words Wouldn't Wait

I've been deep in the work,

trying to perfect the memoir,

laboring over details for days—

but then it came.

A new idea.

A different direction.

Between the memoir

and the thirty-one-day devotional

I had already begun,

another thought rose up:

Use the poems.

Use the essays.

Use what's already alive in you.

Suddenly,

I couldn't think of anything else.

Not the memoir.

Not the devotional.

Just this need

to shape what I already had

into something whole.

Something now.

I was working out this morning,

trying to stay disciplined,

and still—

my mind kept circling back

to structure,

to voice,

to the call

to write it all down.

I tried to push through—

Finish your workout, I told myself.

You know you won't want to come back to it.

But the ideas wouldn't let me go.

So I rushed through it,

heart pounding—

for a reason that had nothing to do with exercise

and everything to do with my thoughts and my words—

and I opened my laptop.

I wrote what I was feeling

right in the moment—

this breathless urgency

to gather the words

before they disappeared.

To capture the rhythm of my soul

before the silence returned.

Now I can't stop

Poems.

Essays.

Prayers.

I keep asking God to guide me,

because I know

this isn't just writing—

it's obedience.

I don't want to forget this moment.

This holy disruption.

This beginning.

If it comes to be,

let it be

because I followed

the pull

and stayed true

to the stirrings of my heart.

I just want

to finish something

and know

that it mattered.

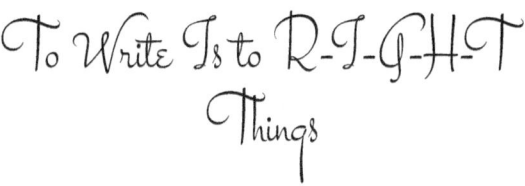

To Write Is to R-I-G-H-T Things

There are moments when my heart can't speak—so it writes.

It pours itself onto the page, because sometimes, that's the only way it knows how to

be heard.

My feelings, overwhelmed by a deep stirring, draw me back to what truly matters.

Fear and doubt, though unwelcome, often come as fire—God's way of refining what's worth keeping and letting the rest fall away.

God moves in His own way, in His own time. And still, we have now—this very breath, this page, this choice to listen deeply to what's stirring inside.

Perhaps the answers aren't beyond us,

but quietly waiting—tucked in the stillness within.

Perhaps the lesson isn't new—

just waiting for us to listen again.

The fever, the stress, the questions—they're forging something sacred, a purpose still unfolding within me.

We weren't called to be perfect.

Perfection is simply our imperfections made sacred through grace and honest effort.

Writing is solitude, yes—

but also dialogue.

With the world.

With the Word.

With ourselves.

The wonders I carry—

and the questions I hold—

are, themselves, the true gifts.

I am part of this moment—fully present—

yet listening from a quiet angle,

watching.

Noticing.

Tuning in to the way the mind moves,

the way the soul responds.

The magic of a quiet evening at home, where hearts touch without words,

feels like the truest kind of wealth.

Yes, this is very true.

Sometimes I feel the gnawing in my heart—

a quiet ache, a restless part,

though I don't have all the answers yet,

I will find them in the process.

Each question—I ponder

And though I stumble, pause, and pray,

the answers bloom along the way.

Heartfelt writing is honest—it speaks truth.

It isn't about pleasing everyone.

It's a sacred communion—

with language,

with silence,

with memory,

with God.

And those I'm meant to journey with—

They will find me.

That's grace.

So I tell the truth—but with compassion.

I strive for excellence, knowing that perfection is a myth.

In finding my true voice—

I simply try to write

good poems,

good prose,

good essays.

God will take care of the rest.

Because when I love it,

I'll keep doing it —

I'll stick with it, for sure.

Because knowing I was created on purpose,

for a purpose—

just like everyone else—

gives every single day meaning.

I love it.

And by the way, this isn't about me—

it's about what I can give.

What I can share that may be of value to others.

I remind myself:

There's nothing more eternal than God's timing—

and I was placed in this moment for a reason.

So I hold on to my voice,

and trust that what I'm doing matters to Him.

When the critic inside begins to stir,

I pause...

and listen for the voice of truth instead.

Maybe you need that reminder too.

You were made for this moment.

So hold on to your voice.

Trust that your doing is more than doing—it's becoming.

And when doubt whispers its lies,

you can still choose to believe what's always been true.

And when I do, I remember that to write is to R-I-G-H-T things:

R – Reveal what's real

I – Invite the Spirit in

G – Give voice to grace

H – Hold space for healing

T – Tell the truth in love

This is the work.

This is the offering.

And this is enough.

SCRIPTURAL ANCHORS

R – Reveal what's real

> *"Let the morning bring me word of your unfailing love, for I have put my trust in you. Show me the way I should go, for to you I entrust my life."*
> — *Psalm 143:8*

Reflection:

Each new morning invites us to begin again—with honesty. When we come before God just as we are, He gently reveals what's real: His unfailing love, His direction, and His trustworthiness in every season.

I – Invite the Spirit in

> *"Whether you turn to the right or to the left, your ears will hear a voice behind you, saying, 'This is the way; walk in it.'"*
> — *Isaiah 30:21*

Reflection:

When we pause to invite the Holy Spirit in, we become attuned to the quiet voice that guides, redirects, and faithfully leads us forward—even when we're unsure of the way.

We never walk alone.

G – Give voice to grace

*"Let your conversation be always full of grace,
    seasoned with salt, so that you may know
    how to answer everyone."*
— *Colossians 4:6*

Reflection:

Our words carry a message. They may carry impact—and with that, opportunity. Speaking with grace doesn't mean avoiding truth, but offering it in a way that reflects the heart of Christ: with kindness, compassion, and love.

H – Hold space for healing

*"These have come so that the proven genuineness
    of your faith—of greater worth than gold,
    which perishes even though refined by fire—
    may result in praise, glory and honor..."*
—*1 Peter 1:7*

Reflection:

Pain has a place in the refining process. When we hold space for our own healing—and that of others—we bear witness to the deeper work of faith, one that shines brighter through surrender than through our own strength.

T – Tell the truth in love

"Instead, speaking the truth in love, we will grow

to become in every respect the mature body of
him who is the head, that is, Christ."
— *Ephesians 4:15*

Reflection:

Truth without love is harsh and can wound. Love without truth is a lie and can withhold freedom. But together, they create space for growth. Speaking the truth in love honors both God's Word and the dignity of those we speak to.

Wit, Wonder, and the Work of Words

A person's true character isn't revealed when all is calm,

but when the winds shift and the ground trembles.

As Douglas Malloch said, "Good timber does not grow with ease; the stronger the wind, the stronger the trees."

It's in those raw, unscripted moments that truth rises—like steam from a fractured stone.

We, too, can rise above our fears, doubts, pain, and grief— and grow from them.

Our emotions, stirred by wonder, can draw us deeper into what we're feeling—

and we can pour our hearts onto paper.

When we write,

we are never alone, though we are solo.

In the quiet, in the stillness, in the beautiful and exhilarating sound of silence—these are sacred moments.

We are in our deepest connection with our thoughts, our feelings, and with God.

From our hearts,

our words are wound together with the invisible threads that bind thought to paper,

soul to soul.

Writing is solitude, yes—

but also dialogue.

With the world.

With the Word.

With ourselves.

I know that—I, and my writing—won't speak to all.

Perhaps not in this season... maybe not even in this generation

But perhaps in the next, or the one after that.

Only God knows. Still, your work may stir a quiet wonder

in someone's soul—

a wonder they didn't know was there

until they heard your voice or read your words

There is strength in that—

in your age,

in the wisdom you've earned,

in the wonder still alive in your eyes.

Let every bit of it empower you—

not in spite of your age,

but because of it.

I'd like to explore the world—

not just with my eyes and feet,

but with my words.

As my grandson says, "I need answers to my wonders"—

and sometimes,

it's the childlike questions that are the true gift,

the ones that spark us to wonder too.

The stirrings of wit and wonder in my soul

are His whispers guiding my pen.

The page may not promise clarity,

but it promises His presence as I write.

And in that presence,

something new always begins.

> *"He has made everything beautiful in its time. He*
> *has also set eternity in the human heart; yet*
> *no one can fathom what God has done from*
> *beginning to end."*
> —*Ecclesiastes 3:11*

PART TWO

Identity, Silence, and the Sacred Unknown

Unapologetically Me

WHY I WRITE

I write because I must.

Writing is how I put my heart into words when my tongue can't.

It's how I release the weight of stress and tension when my soul feels heavy.

It's how I give shape and form to what's burning inside—

so it doesn't consume me,

but instead becomes something I can offer to the world.

I write because it helps me see,

because it helps me pray,

because it helps me heal.

And if, in the end, these words touch even one soul,

then that is grace —

But that's not why I write.

I write because I must.

Writing from the heart is a form of art — yes, a unique expression of words and emotions.

But more than that, it is the language of the soul.

To find answers in the process—not all at once.

Some thoughts are like prayers—

not always spoken, but deeply felt.

Some rise and fade like sighs,

while others settle in my soul

and stay awhile.

But the ones I hold closest

are the quietest ones—

those sacred whispers

that come and go with grace,

leaving behind a lesson,

a nudge,

a trace of God.

Remember... we are all both teachers and students of one another.

Each of us has something to contribute and something to learn—as God guides us.

How awesome is that!

WRITING WITH PURPOSE

There's no room for anxiety when your heart is filled with purpose—bursting with words waiting to come out.

And my purpose is love—for myself, for everybody.

It's a good form of therapy, and hopefully, it's good for others who come across my words.

Purpose expressed fully, intentionally, and without holding back.

Because in the end, it all comes down to love—

and especially in the quiet magic of an ordinary evening at home.

Yes, it's always in the stillness

that these truths rise to the surface.

LEARNING NOT TO GIVE MY POWER AWAY

I'm learning not to give my power away—

to stay rooted in my voice,

to mirror no one but the person God made me to be.

As the old proverb goes:

"Sticks and stones may break my bones, but words will never harm me."

Or could they? Will they?

We do have feelings...

Though praise can comfort me,

criticism can stir my doubt.

So I pause and remember:

they're just words from someone

who sees from a different place—

and I don't always know the reason behind their view.

Not every voice needs a seat at my table.

Not every opinion gets to shape who I become.

And above all—

I'm learning not to take things personally.

What's said about me

often says more about them.

Not everyone will resonate with me. But the ones who do will be part of my journey.

They'll recognize the voice in me.

And I'll recognize theirs too,

simply by speaking with compassion

and trusting God to draw my way the hearts meant to receive it.

FAITHFUL, NOT PERFECT

This isn't about me—

it's about what I can offer, what I can teach, what I can share.

Writing is both solitude and partnership—

a conversation with language, with memory, with God.

I don't need to be perfect—just faithful.

I believe in the value of what I'm doing.

And I will keep writing.

Because when I do—

my heart feels whole,

my words feel alive,

and I remember:

I was created on purpose, for a purpose.

> *"Am I now trying to win the approval of human*
> *beings, or of God? Or am I trying to please*
> *people? If I were still trying to please people, I*
> *would not be a servant of Christ."*
> —*Galatians 1:10*

When Nothing Comes

—A PRAYER FOR WHEN THE WORDS
WON'T COME

My mind draws a blank.

I've been sitting here for hours—

thinking, reading, waiting,

trying to find the right technique,

the secret key

to break through

what they call writer's block.

Is that what this is?

Nothing comes to mind—

though the story is alive inside me.

How do I begin?

What stops me?

What do I fear?

Is it the grammar?

The punctuation?

The rules and rhythms of proper speech?

Or is it the fear of being misunderstood—

or worse,

understood too well?

But I'm writing for myself,

aren't I?

And of course—for You, Lord.

Still...

When I come to know something

deeply,

it never sits lightly—

there's a tug in my heart to pass it on.

So why the silence?

Lord, help me.

Holy Spirit, take over.

Align the words,

align the thoughts,

with what You have planted deep in my heart.

Give them breath.

Give them shape.

Take over, Holy Spirit.

I will listen—

attentively, humbly—

as You whisper

what needs to be shared,

for my good,

and for the good

of anyone who's willing to listen.

So here I am, Lord—

pen in hand,

heart open,

ready to begin.

Amen.

> "Then the Lord replied: 'Write down the
>   revelation and make it plain on tablets so that
>   a herald may run with it."
> —Habakkuk 2:2

Here I Am Again, Lord

Here I am again, Lord.

After another dry spell where nothing comes—no fresh words, no burning thought or stirring feeling. Just silence.

How am I to finish what I've begun when I hit these long, quiet stretches? I know You called me to write, to tell the story You planted in me. But sometimes the pages stay blank, and my spirit feels both restless and sleepy.

Still, this longing won't let go.

I want to finish a book. Even just one.

To complete it, hold it in my hands, run my fingers over the cover and pages and whisper, "We did it, Lord."

A work poured out in trust, every word a small act of obedience and hope.

So here I am.

Asking, again.

For a spark.

A whisper.

A feeling.

Something. Anything.

And yet, maybe this moment—this very ache, this hunger for the next word—is the beginning of the next page. Maybe I don't need a flood of inspiration, just the faith to show up with pen in hand and heart open wide.

Maybe it's okay to write from the in-between.

To trust that even the dry spells are soaked in Your presence.

To believe that the silence holds the promise of a whisper.

Speak, Lord.

Even a word is enough.

The Tremors That Test Our Roots

"When anxiety was great within me,
your consolation brought me joy."
— *Psalm 94:19*

I was overwhelmed.

The words sprinted onto the page—

I didn't chase them.

I let them run wild until they grew quiet

and formed something sacred.

Because stress may trigger the outburst,

but perspective filters the grace.

Character isn't shaped by ease.

It's revealed when the wind howls,

when we're rattled to the core,

when the storm calls us by name.

These are the tremors that test our roots.

What do we do when we can't stop shaking?

We dig deeper. We lean in.

We whisper Scripture into the quake.

We write our way through.

Even then, there's hope:

"There are blessings in every curse," someone once said.

And I've learned to believe it.

Responding to God's Constant Nudge

I wrote this piece at the very beginning of the year, at the realization that I would soon turn seventy—before I had any clear plans for this book—or any book. Looking back now, reading it as part of my completed manuscript, I'm overcome with emotion. Every word has come to life, reminding me of how it all began.

What was once just a quiet nudge has become a living testimony of God's faithfulness.

This is where I paused and finally obeyed the nudge.

This is my testimony of a journey I never planned.

This is where the journey started.

* * *

Something long dormant in me is beginning to surface—a desire to start something and see it through.

I want to leave a legacy that my loved ones and friends can hold on to long after I'm gone. I feel a strong desire to awaken

the writer within me and create something tangible they can return to—a poem, a memoir, or perhaps even a novel.

I want to write as if God Himself is guiding every word, as if He's whispering it to me. I know I'll need all of His help and support.

I don't want my words to simply be read—I want them to be felt. I hope that when my children, grandchildren, great-grandchildren,

and friends come across my writing one day, they'll hear my voice between the lines. That they'll sense God's presence in the pauses,

the prayers, and the stories I leave behind. I want them to know who I was—not just through memories, but through words that point

them to something greater than me.

Writing has always felt sacred to me, even when I wasn't actively doing it. Now, more than ever, I feel an urgency—not of pressure,

but of purpose. I believe God has been gently preparing me

for this, planting seeds over the years. And now, it's time to water them.

I don't want to do this alone. I want to write with God—not just about Him, but with Him. I want each word to come from a place of prayer,

each sentence to carry the weight of something eternal. Sometimes I imagine myself sitting quietly, pen in hand, listening... waiting for

His voice. And when I hear it—whether it comes as a memory, a phrase, or just a sense of peace—I want to write it down with reverence.

There's no doubt I'll need His help—every step of the way. I don't know exactly what I'll write yet, or how it will unfold. But I do know this:

I want to be faithful to His nudge. To the calling. To the desire that's been quietly growing in me all these years.

So I begin—with open hands and an open heart. I may not know exactly what the finished work will look like, but I know the One who does.

I trust that if I keep showing up—prayerful, willing, and surrendered—God will meet me there. He'll give me the words. He'll guide the process.

And if, one day, those words find their way into the hands of someone I love—or even a stranger—and they feel comforted, inspired,

or even drawn closer to Him—then that will be enough. That will be my offering. That will be my legacy.

May this be the season my writer-self begin to bloom.

> *"For it is God who works in you to will and to act*
> *in order to fulfill his good purpose."*
> —*Philippians 2:13*

REFLECTION

The desire to write, to create, to leave a legacy—none of it begins with us alone. It is God who plants the longing and gives us both the will and the strength to bring it to life, all for His good purpose.

When Joy Isn't Shared

Sadly, sometimes, after a long and meaningful journey— just as the path begins to come together—we discover that not everyone will share our joy. Yet still, we learn to carry our joy with grace.

Not everyone will celebrate the things that bring us joy.

Some will stand at a distance when our lives begin to bloom—

not wanting to give us the satisfaction of their validation—

not out of resentment, but perhaps from the ache of their own unspoken longing.

It can be disheartening when those who've known our past

can't seem to meet us in the joy of the present—

especially when the moment is sacred:

a quiet or unexpected dream finally taking form.

Sometimes, we extend an invitation out of kindness,

never expecting it to be accepted—

only hoping the gesture might be received with warmth.

But when the response comes sharp or dismissive,

it's not just the words that wound—

it's the absence of shared joy.

In those moments, we learn to hold our joy anyway.

To carry it with reverence, even if others do not.

To trust that it was never meant to be validated by approval,

but rooted in something deeper—

the quiet assurance that we are walking in step

with the One who sees the whole story.

So we release the need to be understood,

to be joined or affirmed—

and instead, we celebrate anyway.

Still grateful.

Still graceful.

Still whole.

> *"You make known to me the path of life; you will*
> *fill me with joy in your presence,*
> *with eternal pleasures at your right hand."*
> *—Psalm 16:1*

REFLECTION

Not everyone will understand or celebrate our joy—but that doesn't make it any less real. God fills us with joy in His presence, and that joy remains full, even when it's not shared.

I Don't Have Time to Not Have Time

"I don't have time to not have time."

The words came unexpectedly—and struck with impact.

And the more I sat with them, the more I understood:

It wasn't just a passing thought.

It was a loud, holy interruption.

A gentle nudge from God.

A reminder that this—

this season,

this stirring,

this still-beating heart—

is not to be wasted.

For too long, I told myself I needed more:

More time.

More clarity.

More understanding of how to begin.

More material to fill the pages.

But what I really needed... was to just start.

Not because I had it all figured out

Not because I finally felt "ready."

But because the desire to write, to reflect, to pass something on—that desire hasn't let go of me.

And I've come to believe it isn't just mine.

It's God's.

This book—whether it becomes one of many or the only one I leave behind—is an offering:

A legacy

of presence,

of quiet obedience,

of trust.

There's a sacred responsibility in sharing what God has placed within me—

and a sacred release in finally letting it go into the world.

So here I am.

Writing with what I have.

Honoring what I know.

Trusting that God will use it—

in whatever ways it may be an encouragement to others...

Maybe you're reading this because you've felt something similar—

a pull to start,

a weight in your heart,

a whisper you can't shake.

Let me encourage you:

You don't have time to not have time either.

So don't wait.

Begin.

> *"Whoever watches the wind will not plant;*
> *whoever looks at the clouds will not reap."*
> —*Ecclesiastes 11:4*

REFLECTION

If we wait for perfect conditions, we may never begin. God calls us to trust Him with what we have now—to plant, to write, to act—and let Him bring the harvest in His time.

Whisper to Me, Lord

"The Sovereign Lord has given me a well-
instructed tongue,
to know the word that sustains the weary.
He wakens me morning by morning,
wakens my ear to listen like one being instructed."
— *Isaiah 50:4*

Whisper to me, Lord,

and help me form Your vision into words.

I so long to share Your words with the world—

especially with those who will listen.

Help us. Shape us.

Open our hearts and minds,

and let Your words and teaching

permeate in and beyond our soul.

We all need a nudge—a word here and there from You—

though some may not recognize that it is You.

Please open and soften their hearts

to receive and understand Your word,

so they may tuck it in their hearts,

even if not for today,

but for some day

when they will need to hear it.

Soften their hearts, Lord.

And may they locate those words of Yours—

tucked away somewhere in their hearts—

when they need them most.

Amen.

PART THREE

My Heart's Echo for Others

These prayers, poems, and reflections are filled with the love I feel for those who've touched my life—whether family, friend, or stranger. They hold my emotions—sometimes with tears, sometimes in joy, often in awe.

Each piece is an echo of something God placed on my heart—now finally released, with hope it will comfort, encourage, or speak truth in the life of another.

I Don't Think I Can...

And yet, that's where the bravest journeys begin.

Dedicated to anyone who thinks they can't do it—

Can't begin.

Can't start over.

Can't change course.

Especially to the young ones still trying to figure out what life is all about,

and to those who are young at heart—

who, somewhere along the way, have come to the false and absurd conclusion that it's too late.

Too late to dream again.

Too late to start something new.

Too late to discover who they really are.

Here I am, starting anew.

I've started and paused at different stages of my life.

I used to call them failures—

but truthfully, I didn't fail.

I just didn't follow through.

Life got in the way.

You know what I mean...

But here's what I've learned:

Find your passion—something you love to do—

and the skills will follow.

For some, they may simply surface,

already within you, ready to rise.

Sometimes they're skills you never even knew you had.

Try something new.

Because if you don't try,

you'll never know.

Once you find your niche—

the thing that sparks your joy—

you'll keep doing it.

And that doing will become part of your healing.

It will bring you joy and meaning.

Look for it. Find it.

If you discover it early in life—what a blessing.

But if you don't?

It's still not too late.

Try anyway. Try always.

You just might surprise yourself.

> *"I can do all this through him who gives me strength."*
> — *Philippians 4:13*

REFLECTION

Strength to begin, to try, to dream again—it doesn't come from us alone. It comes from Christ, who supplies all we need to take the first step and every step after.

The Loudness of Silence

"Be still, and know that I am God."
— Psalm 46:10

There's a sound to stillness—

if you dare to listen.

There is beauty in a hushed atmosphere.

I can hear myself think.

I can feel myself feel

All the outside noise is blocked out,

and I can truly understand myself.

Hallelujah!

To be one with myself—

one with God.

To meditate.

To pray.

To reflect—

on my feelings,

on the days past,

on today,

and on the days ahead.

What a most precious gift this is.

Seize it.

Very seldom do we have the time.

So when it comes, grab hold of it.

Don't hesitate.

We not only need clarity—

we deserve it.

This is not just a good prescription;

it's the absolute cure

to feel whole.

So make time, dear ones.

This is absolutely crucial

for our hearts

and for our minds.

My Great Escape

This piece began as a journal entry sometime in 1996. Later that year, I was asked to write an assignment for class using descriptive language. I recreated that journal entry from memory, incorporating the imagery I was learning to use.

The version included in this collection is that very assignment—rediscovered after almost three decades later, even though many of my journals have been lost or let go. In many ways, this piece found its way back to me, and I felt led to include it here. I'm trusting it will find its way to whoever needs it now.

There is a place I love to go whenever I am feeling down, or simply tired and bored. It is a small, warm, cozy space, beautifully decorated in cool shades of mauve and pale blue. The room isn't very large and doesn't really have any furniture, except for a big, soft, cushiony emerald-green pillow, which I comfortably plop onto as soon as I arrive. A couple of my favorite paintings—by Monet and Matisse—hang on one wall, blending soothingly with the room's colors.

Soft, relaxing music is always playing as I come in. The place is surrounded by a small, blue lake and beautiful flowers and trees. It is quiet and peaceful. When the doors and windows are open, I can hear the birds chirping and singing and smell the freshness of the air drifting in.

It is a serene place where I can quiet my mind and do absolutely nothing but sit, enjoy the surroundings, and be with God. Here, I can think any thoughts I want, without anyone or anything to interrupt me.

With the beauty and peace of this place, I end up thinking very pleasant thoughts—or nothing at all—and feel a calming effect wash over me.

The best part?

I always have access to this peaceful place of mine anytime I want, no matter where I am. I never have to rush to get there, for it is located in a precious and sacred space—within my heart and mind—and I can summon it whenever I need to get away and center myself.

This is my great escape.

> *"Yes, my soul, find rest in God; my hope comes*
> *from him."*
> *—Psalm 62:5*

Grateful, Yet Grieving (Devotional)

There are moments when I sit with both gratitude and sorrow—thankful for all God has done in my life, and yet aching for others who do not know Him.

I think of the faces I see in passing—those burdened with anxiety, weariness, or a sadness they've grown used to carrying. I wonder how they go on day after day. How do they endure without the hope of Christ? I know I can't fix everything or everyone, but sometimes I wish I could.

Still, I trust that God sees them, loves them more than I ever could, and knows the timing and path for each heart. And so I pray:

Lord, how can I be a blessing? How can You use me to reflect Your light and love into their lives?

Some will be reached. Some will stay stuck. But I believe You're still working, still whispering, still pursuing. Teach me to walk with compassion, not despair—to hold space for others without being crushed by the weight of their pain.

Thank You for the peace You've planted in me. Help me sow it where You lead.

> "The Lord is not slow in keeping his promise... He is patient with you, not wanting anyone to perish, but everyone to come to repentance."
> —2 Peter 3:9

* * *

The same heart, now in verse.

GRATEFUL, YET GRIEVING (POEM)

There are moments

when I sit

with both gratitude and sorrow—

thankful for all God has done in my life,

and yet aching

for those who do not know Him.

I see them in passing—

faces drawn with weariness,

eyes heavy with unseen battles,

shoulders slumped beneath

a sadness they've learned to carry.

And I wonder...

How do they go on

without the hope of Christ?

How do they wake,

and work,

and wait,

never knowing

they are deeply loved?

I can't fix it all.

I know that.

But sometimes,

my heart still breaks

wishing I could.

Yet I trust

that God sees them—

every unspoken ache,

every restless night,

every silent plea

they don't know is a prayer.

He loves them

more than I ever could.

He knows the timing,

the path,

the turning point.

So I ask Him—

Lord, how can I be a blessing?

How can You use me

to reflect Your light,

Your love,

into their lives?

Some will be reached.

Some will stay stuck.

Still, You are working.

Still, You are whispering.

Still, You are pursuing.

Teach me to walk

with compassion, not despair—

to hold space for others

without being crushed

by the weight of their pain.

Thank You

for the peace You've planted in me.

Help me

sow it

where You lead.

A PRAYER

Lord, thank You for saving me, for the unshakable hope I have in You. My heart aches for those who don't yet know Your love. Show me how to bless them—not by fixing them, but by reflecting You. Keep my spirit soft, my prayers steady, and my eyes open to those You place in my path. Amen.

PART FOUR

Generations and Grace

A Young Voice, A Timeless Truth

*"From the lips of children and infants you, Lord,
have called forth your praise?"*
—Matthew 21:16

God often speaks through the unexpected—like the thoughtful voice of my nine-year-old grandson.

One afternoon, I asked him to make something for me, and as he worked on his project, I heard him murmur under his breath:

"You can't rush perfection..."

That small comment stopped me in my tracks.

So I invited him to share what he felt about perfection, and I wrote it down as he spoke. What he shared became the poem that follows.

In his words, I saw not only his heart—but also a glimpse of God's gentle reminder:

Perfection isn't the goal. Faithfulness is.

You Can't Rush Perfection

A POETIC CONVERSATION BETWEEN MY GRANDSON AND ME

GRANDSON

You can't rush perfection...

But you can sign up for success and show up for it every day.

And if you don't succeed the first time, you can try again.

But just know that nothing is really perfect.

You can try and try... they may be great, but they will never be perfect.

Because they say perfection is a myth... and myths are not true.

However, we can still strive to be perfect,

But it's a relief to know that nothing is really perfect.

GRANDMOTHER

And even in the trying, we are growing.

Success begins with showing up with heart.

Grace meets us in our "almosts."

It's okay to be unfinished—we're all still becoming.

Faithfulness, not flawlessness, is what God delights in.

What a relief, indeed.

For My Great-Grandchildren

SJ, NEVEAH, PERSEUS, VIDA, AND THE LITTLE
ONE WE'RE JOYFULLY WAITING TO MEET

*"Start children off on the way they should go,
and even when they are old they will not turn
from it."*
—Proverbs 22:6

Each of you holds a piece of my heart.

I never imagined I'd be a great grandma—

what a joy and honor that is.

You are each a gift—

a tender whisper of God's goodness,

a surprise blessing I didn't even know to pray for...

and yet, here you are.

As you grow, I pray you grow strong in faith,

gentle in spirit, and confident in who God made you to be.

May you love the Lord with all your heart, soul, mind, and strength,

and walk closely with Him through every season of your life.

May His hand guide you,

His voice speak to you,

and His love surround you—

now and always.

With all my love and prayers,

Lola

For My Granddaughter, Nini

*"She is clothed with strength and dignity; she can
laugh at the days to come."*
—*Proverbs 31:25*

From the moment I first saw you, I knew—

God had answered a quiet prayer tucked deep within my heart.

You are grace in motion.

You are joy wrapped in possibility.

Each time I see you, you've grown—taller, wiser, more radiant.

It takes my breath away.

I'm always thankful for those few brief, beautiful glimpses.

I treasure them all.

I speak your name often in my prayers.

May you become a woman whose beauty is more than what's seen—

A woman marked by kindness, courage, wisdom,

and the kind of faith that changes lives.

I may not always be near.

But God always is.

And that, baby girl, is enough.

With all my love and prayers,

Lola Joji

For My Younger Grandsons

JONAS, DONOVAN, APOLLO, AND AUGUST

> *"Be devoted to one another in love.*
> *Honor one another above yourselves."*
> *—Romans 12:10*

What joy it is to see you—especially when you're side by side.

You may not realize it now, but the bond you share is a gift.

Each time I witness it, my heart overflows with hope and gratitude.

I pray that your love for one another not only grows—

but deepens with time.

That you'll learn to lean on each other,

look out for each other,

and never take for granted the strength of brotherhood.

I pray you'll grow into strong, kind, faith-filled young men—

men who honor God with their lives,

who love deeply, live wisely, and walk in truth.

I ask God to bless you with every good thing.

May His wisdom guide your choices,

His presence surround your days,

and His love be the anchor that holds you steady

when the world feels uncertain.

I love you all so much.

And when there's more I wish I could do for you,

I trust and rest in knowing:

God can—when I cannot.

With all my love and prayers,

Lola

For My Older Grandchildren

KENNETH AND LOANN, VANESSA AND SUA, JOSHUA AND ISIS, AND KIANA

"But from everlasting to everlasting
the Lord's love is with those who fear him,
and his righteousness with their children's
*   children."*
—*Psalm 103:17*

Each of you is such an incredible blessing.

I love you more than words can ever express.

I pray you'll always be seekers of truth—

lovers of learning, lovers of life, and lovers of God.

May you grow ever more into the people you were created to be—

wise, compassionate, and grounded in what is good and lasting.

May you walk closely with the Lord,

even when the path feels steep.

May He guide your every step,

protect your hearts,

comfort your sorrows,

and stay beside you when I cannot.

You are always in my prayers,

always in my heart.

And I thank the Lord for each of you—

every single day.

With all my love and prayers,

Lola

For My Children

VICTOR AND CATHERINE, DAWN AND JUSTIN,
JOHN AND SHIELA, AND LEA

> *"The Lord bless you and keep you; the Lord make*
> *his face shine on you and be gracious to you;*
> *the Lord turn his face toward you and give*
> *you peace."*
> —*Numbers 6:24–26*

Each of you is an incredible blessing—

in more ways than words can fully express.

I see it in the love you share,

the way you show up for your families,

and the strength and grace with which you live each day.

Vic and Cat—your devotion to your children and grand-
children is wholehearted and admirable.

Dawn and Justin—your energy, patience, and constant presence in the lives of your boys speak volumes.

John and Shiela—the way you've nurtured and encouraged your daughter's gifts has been a joy to witness.

And Lea—your love for your nieces, nephews, grandnieces, and grandnephews

does not go unnoticed, nor unappreciated.

The love you have for one another

is one of the greatest gifts a mother could ever hope for.

I pray that God continues to surround you

with His covering of grace—

an umbrella of love, comfort, protection, and wisdom—

and every other good thing

only a mother longs to ask and pray for.

I love you all so much.

With all my love and prayers,

Mom

PART FIVE

Love That Lasts

For My Husband, Danny

WHO IS TRULY THE BETTER HALF OF OUR RELATIONSHIP

"A faithful person will be richly blessed..."
— *Proverbs 28:20*

You are one of a kind.

Your spirit is full of fun, love, compassion, honesty, generosity, and patience.

Your wisdom and helpfulness are a guiding light to everyone who knows you.

You are a blessing to many.

And to me... a daily gift.

My life would not be what it is today without your genuine support—

so unselfish with your time, allowing me the space just to be.

Because of that, I never had to set aside what matters most to me:

having my quiet time.

Thank you for always honoring that space—

whenever I need it, or simply want it—

and for that, I am truly grateful.

Words could never fully capture the depth of my love or gratitude for who you are.

I love you with all my heart and being.

I pray God's richest blessings for you—

that He would continue to grant you strength, wisdom, compassion,

and every good thing He has already so generously poured into your life.

Because we are the ones who are truly blessed...

to have you in ours.

With all my love and prayers,

Joji

PART SIX

Seasoned Grace

Seventy, Finally!

I feel blessed.

I feel good.

I feel sad.

I feel guilty.

God has been so good to me—

do I deserve it?

Sometimes I wish I had trillions,

a magic wand in hand—

not just to give,

but to fix what's broken,

to pour love where it's missing,

to heal where there is illness,

to take away every pain.

But only God has the power to do that.

So I pray that my love and my prayers are enough—

because that is where my true riches are stored.

I never dreamed I'd make it this far.

My life has been far from perfect—

but in its own way,

a beautiful kind of imperfect perfection.

I am truly blessed.

> *"Even to your old age and gray hairs I am he, I*
> *am he who will sustain you.*
> *I have made you and I will carry you; I will*
> *sustain you and I will rescue you."*
> *—Isaiah 46:4*

Sacred Traces at 70

Wrinkles, crow's feet, bags—and oh, those lines:

A line on the left,

A line on the right,

A line going up,

A line going down,

A cluster by my eyes—

from years of smiling—and yes, rubbing—

and crisscrossed lines everywhere.

A bike fall carved its mark on my right,

while my left moved on with quiet lines.

A little more each day—

a bounty gathered through the years.

Each one is a sign

of a God-given gift to me:

Hard and meaningful work,

Deep thoughts,

Happy times,

Sad times,

Stressful times,

Funny times.

Each new line and wrinkle

is one step closer to God.

Gray hair?

It's wisdom's way, blooming at my roots—

a sign I've lived,

a gentle reminder that I'm still growing,

still learning,

still held,

still His.

On aches and pain:

One day is better than some,

another is worse than most.

Some days are good.

Some days are tough.

If God is keeping me here,

He's not done with me yet.

Some days,

the aches speak louder than my joy—

but I remind myself:

Every ache,

every wrinkle,

is one step closer to God.

So I take it...

one day,

one ache at a time—

by His grace.

"Therefore we do not lose heart.
Though outwardly we are wasting away,
yet inwardly we are being renewed day by day."
—2 Corinthians 4:16

PART SEVEN

A Final Blessing

A Closing Benediction

To every heart who turned these pages with openness and grace—my sincerest thank you.

I pray these words brought you comfort.

And if they did,

may they linger in your quiet moments.

If they stirred questions,

may you carry them to the Lord who welcomes your wonder.

If they reminded you of beauty,

may you learn to notice it more often—in the small, in the still, in the sacred.

You don't need to have it all figured out.

You don't need to rush.

You don't need to be perfect.

You are loved—as you are,

right here, right now.

May you find peace in the pauses.

Purpose in the process.

And joy in the journey.

May you draw near to God in the stillness

and find that He has been near to you all along.

Until we meet again,

may His grace hold you,

His whisper guide you,

and His light shine between the lines of your own story.

With all my heart,

Joy G. Arcayena

"Come near to God and he will come near to you."
— *James 4:8*

A Quiet Moment of Reflection

As you close these pages, may you carry forward the stillness, the hope, and the whisper of grace found between the lines.

* * *

A companion to your journey through

Light Between the Lines: Finding God in the Quiet Spaces

Take a moment to pause. Let your heart settle. As you close this book, may these gentle prompts invite you into deeper reflection with the One who has been with you all along.

REFLECTIVE PROMPT

What has God whispered to you in the quiet spaces between these lines?

Let this book be more than words—it is a sacred invitation to notice, to listen, and to remember.

JOURNALING QUESTIONS

What piece or passage resonated with you the most? Why?

Have you noticed a shift in how you view silence, waiting, or spiritual nudges?

Is there something God is inviting you to begin, release, or revisit?

What quiet space in your own life might be waiting to bloom?

Again,

THANK YOU FOR JOINING ME IN THESE PAGES.

May your quiet spaces draw you ever closer to the One who lovingly knows and fully sees you.

Acknowledgments

I could never have brought this book to life without the loving support and encouragement of the people God so graciously placed in my life. To my beloved family, relatives, dear friends, and faithful prayer partners—thank you for cheering me on and lifting me up in prayer. To the writing coaches, mentors, and faith-filled authors—whether we've met in person or your words reached me from afar—you helped awaken the writer in me, and I am forever grateful.

I am especially thankful to Scott Alvord and Bessie Nguyen, whose timely support carried me through the most challenging part of this journey: the technical side! To Jennifer Crosswhite and the team at Tandem Services LLC —thank you for your insight, encouragement, and care. I am also deeply grateful for the skilled editors, proofreaders, formatters, and illustrators behind the scenes whose excellence helped shape this work with beauty and grace.

A special thanks to Madelyn Copperwaite, my gifted cover designer, who so beautifully captured the heart of this book, and to my amazing launch team and ARC readers, whose early encouragement, feedback, and support helped carry this message into the world with joy. And to every person who ever told me, *"You should start writing again,"* know that this book carries the echo of your encouragement.

Above all, to God be the glory—for every word written, every lesson learned, and every life this book may reach.

With heartfelt thanks,

Joy

Afterword

From the Author

This isn't just a faith book. It's a human one.

Though rooted in Scripture and written openly from my Christian perspective, *Light Between the Lines*: Finding God in the Quiet Spaces is for anyone wrestling with questions of purpose, identity, and hope—regardless of where you stand in your faith.

At 70, I've returned to writing from the heart after decades of business writing and silent pages. These words don't come with all the answers—but they do come from a life that has lived through the questions.

For me, it's a journey of writing. But for you, I hope it's something familiar—something that meets you right where you are, in whatever season or situation you're walking through.

If you don't know me personally, I hope you'll still hear my heart in these pages. And maybe—just maybe—you'll hear something of your own story too.

It's never too late—or too early—to start reading between the lines.

— Joy G. Arcayena

About the Author

Joy G. Arcayena is a writer, wife, mother, grandmother, and great-grandmother who returned to her love of writing after decades of living, working, and quietly collecting life stories along the way. Now in her 70s, she writes from a place of faith, reflection, and hard-earned wisdom—inviting others to find God in the quiet spaces of their own lives. *Light Between the Lines: Finding God in the Quiet Spaces* is her debut collection of memoir, essays, poetry, and prayerful reflections—written straight from the heart and rooted in grace.

Connect with Joy

joygarcayena@gmail.com

Instagram: @joygarcayenawrites